Jobs and Artificial Intelligence

Haley Williams

childsworld.com

The Child's World
childsworld.com

Published by The Child's World®
800-599-READ • www.childsworld.com

Photography Credits
Photographs ©: Shutterstock Images, cover, 1, 5, 6, 11, 13, 14, 17, 19; Adrian Mars/Shutterstock Images, 9; Sundry Photography/Shutterstock Images, 21; Design elements from Tatiana Shepeleva/Shutterstock Images and Shutterstock Images

ISBN Information
9781503893818 (Reinforced Library Binding)
9781503894631 (Portable Document Format)
9781503895454 (Online Multi-user eBook)
9781503896277 (Electronic Publication)

LCCN 2024941401

Printed in the United States of America

BRINGING THE WORLD TO YOUNG READERS 1968

ABOUT THE AUTHOR

Haley Williams is an editor who lives in Minnesota. In her free time, she enjoys reading, taking walks, and watching movies.

CONTENTS

CHAPTER ONE

ROBOT WAITERS

Marcus and Serena went to a restaurant for dinner. The restaurant had just opened, and the two friends were excited to try it out. A robot stood by the door. When the friends walked inside, the robot said, “Welcome!” They had never been greeted by a robot before.

A human hostess took the friends to a table. The hostess told Marcus and Serena to use the tablet on the table to order food and drinks. Marcus took the tablet and scrolled through the menu. He tapped on the drink and sandwich he wanted. A screen came up recommending appetizers. Marcus thought the chips and salsa looked tasty. He added them to the order.

Serena picked what she wanted. Then she sent their order to the kitchen. A few minutes later, a robot stopped at their table. It carried several trays of food. On the trays were their food and drinks. Serena and Marcus grabbed their food.

Some restaurants around the world use robot waiters to serve their customers.

After the trays were clear, the robot said, "Enjoy!" Then it turned and rolled back to the kitchen. The robot weaved around the tables. When someone walked in front of the robot, it stopped to let the person pass. Marcus and Serena were impressed by the robot's humanlike behavior. The robot was able to act this way thanks to artificial intelligence (AI).

AI is technology that allows computers and machines to do things that are normally only done by people. Robot waiters are one example of AI technology. These **automated** robots have **sensors** that tell them when food is on their trays. The robots also use those sensors to avoid running into tables and people. Restaurants can use AI in other ways, too. For example, AI can suggest menu items to customers.

Many **industries** use AI. The technology saves time and money for companies. It can make certain tasks easier and more **efficient**. Some workers are using AI at their jobs. Other workers are being replaced by AI. And some people are working to improve AI. Although it is still a growing technology, AI is already having a big effect on jobs.

Sensors allow AI-powered robots to perform precise tasks on goods being produced in factories.

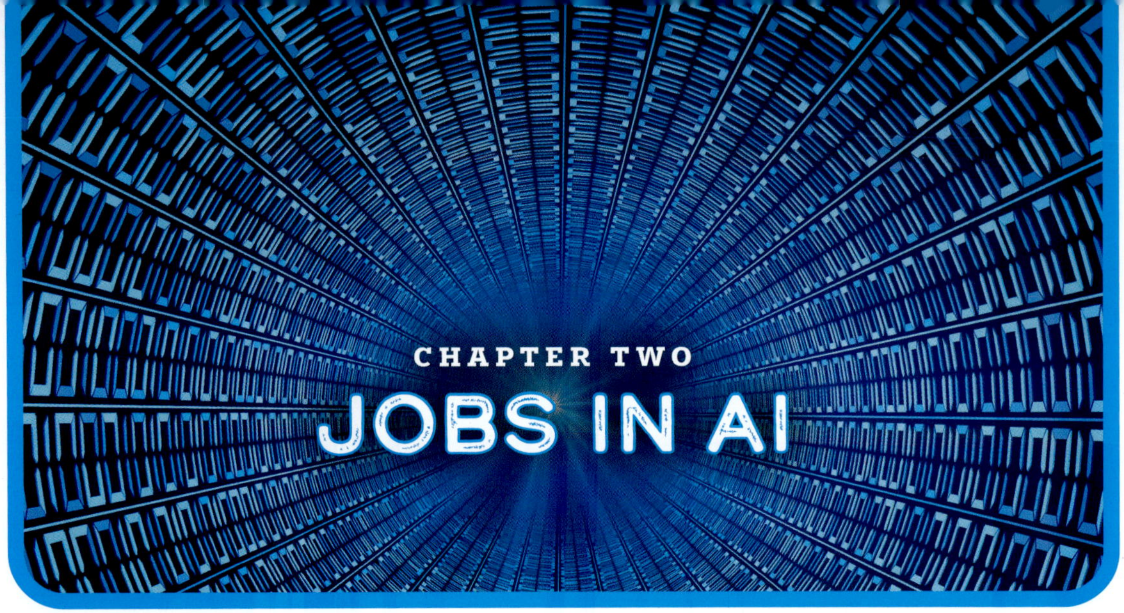

CHAPTER TWO

JOBS IN AI

AI has come a long way from its beginnings. In the 1950s, computer scientist Alan Turing introduced the idea of AI. He wondered whether machines could think as humans do. Since then, people have done a lot of work to develop AI. Modern computer scientists are still working to improve the technology's abilities.

There are many jobs people can get in AI. Some people are AI developers. AI developers are people who use computer programming to create AI systems. AI developers often work with companies to find ways to use AI. The developers create **algorithms** that let AI systems process information.

Turing helped build a computer that Great Britain used to read secret German messages during World War II (1939–1945). This computer (modeled above) looked much different than modern computers.

Other people who work in AI are machine learning **engineers**. Machine learning is a type of AI. It uses **data** and algorithms to help AI improve itself and make decisions on its own. Machine learning engineers create and maintain AI programs. They give these programs lots of data. The programs study the data and find patterns in it. That way, the programs can solve problems when given new data.

Data scientists collect and **analyze** data, usually for companies. They often use machine learning to find patterns in the data they have collected. In addition, data scientists use AI to make predictions about future events, such as how many sales a company can expect to make. These predictions can help companies make better business decisions.

ROBOTICS AND AI

Robotics is a field in which people design and program robots to perform tasks. The robotics industry uses AI to give robots new abilities. Machine learning helps make this possible. Robots use machine learning to help them learn how to solve new problems. Machine learning also allows robots to make their own decisions while performing tasks. Some companies use AI-powered robots in factories to create products.

Computers cannot understand regular human languages the way people can. Programming languages are designed to be understood by computers.

People with jobs in AI usually need to have good math skills. They often need to know programming languages. These languages allow programmers to tell computers what to do. Some of the most common programming languages used in AI are Python and Java.

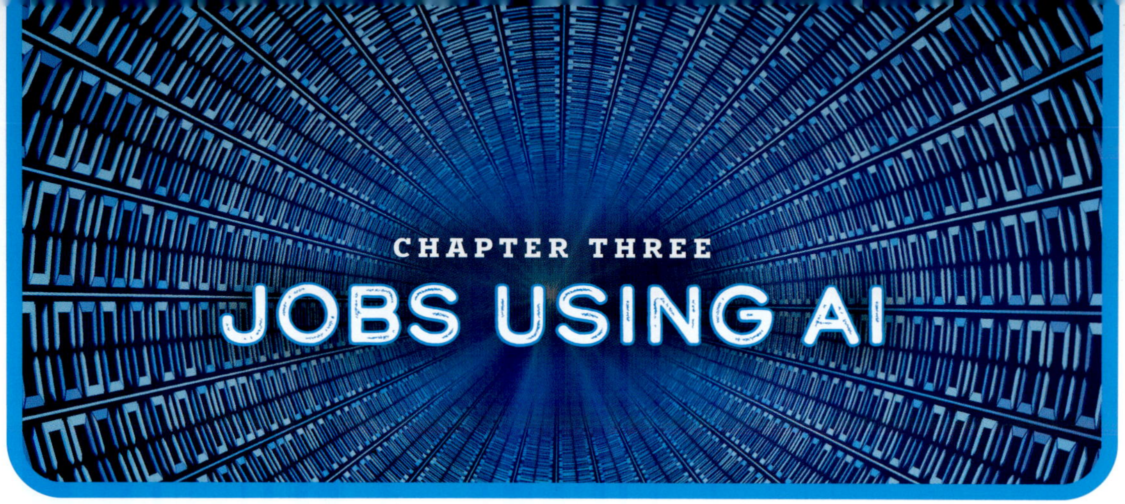

CHAPTER THREE

JOBS USING AI

AI technology has become an important tool in many industries. Businesses can use AI to make doing everyday tasks easier and faster. AI also can help people in more complicated ways. Industries are finding more ways to use AI as the technology improves.

Health care is one industry that uses AI. For example, some doctors use AI to help **diagnose** medical conditions. Doctors diagnose conditions by studying patients, running tests, and looking at scans. Then they use their knowledge to decide what might be causing a patient's condition. AI can help doctors with this task. Doctors can put test results, scans, and other data into an AI system. The AI system has learned from many other diagnoses in the past. It lists possible diseases that could be affecting a patient. This allows the doctors to make more informed decisions.

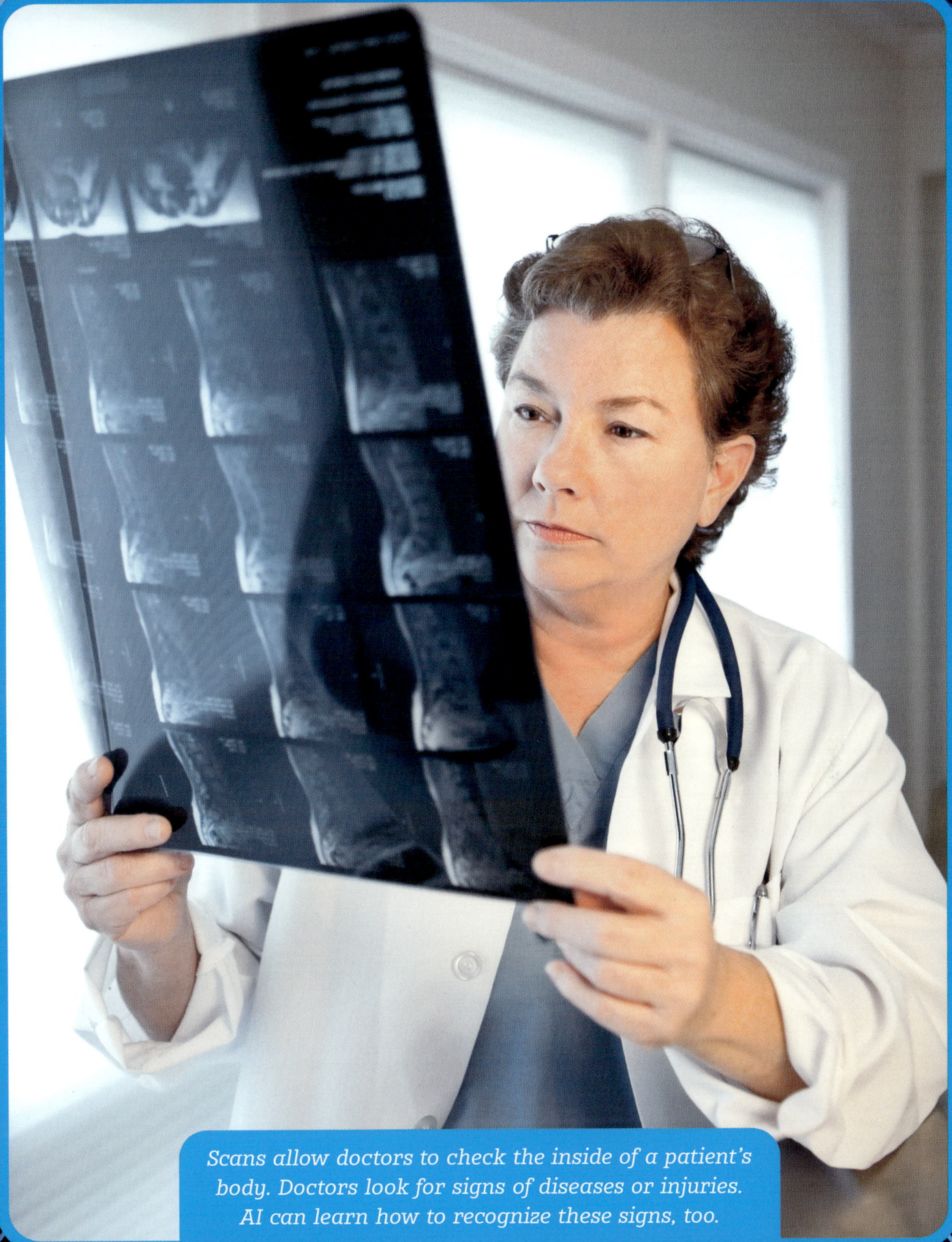

Scans allow doctors to check the inside of a patient's body. Doctors look for signs of diseases or injuries. AI can learn how to recognize these signs, too.

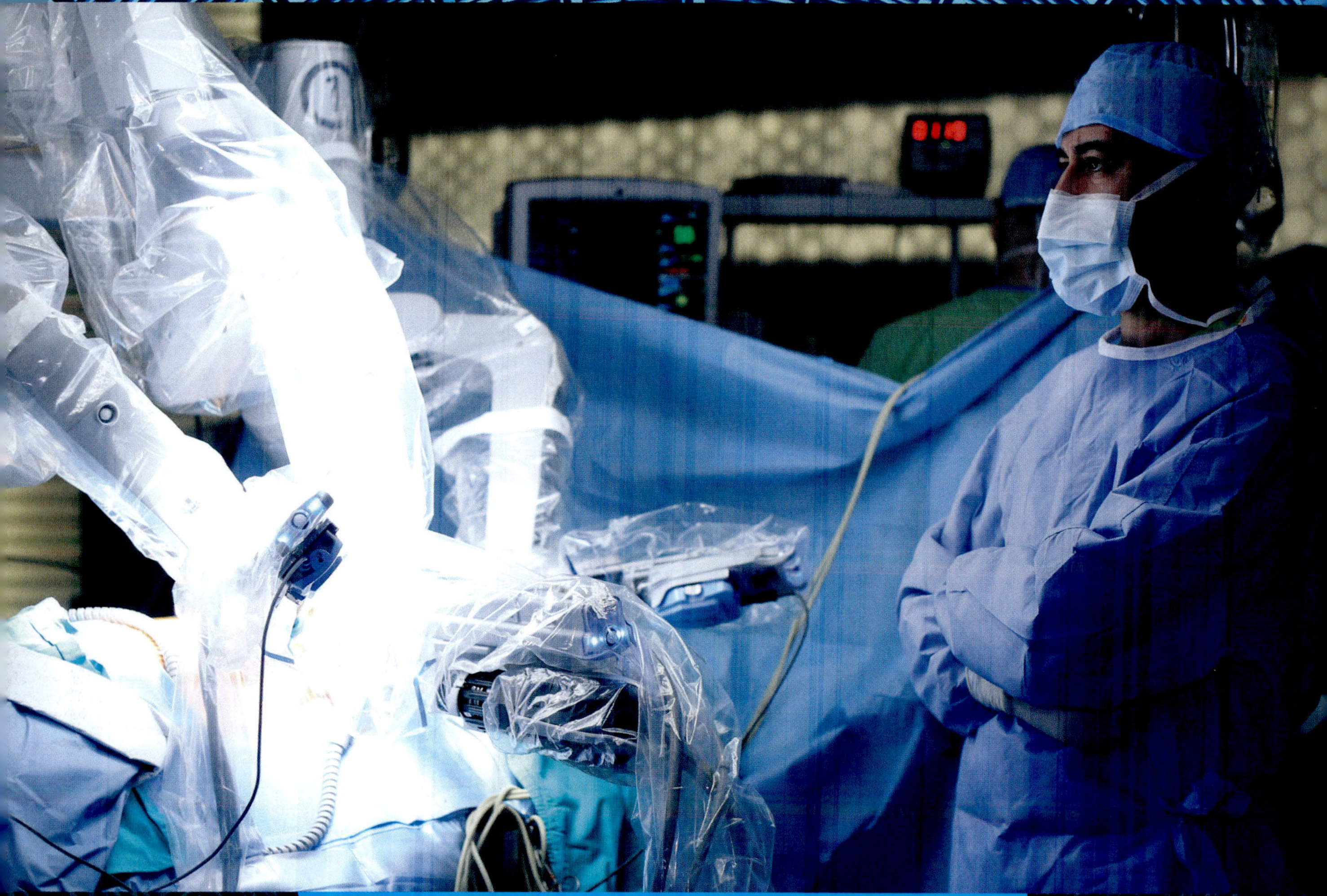

Doctors have used robots in surgery for decades. Advances in AI may allow robots to help doctors even further.

Experts expect AI to help doctors in surgery, too. Doctors sometimes use robots during surgery. Some robotic devices have cameras that record surgeries. AI could analyze the information in the video. It could then suggest next steps during a tricky surgery. It could also notice something that a doctor might have missed.

AI is used in banking as well. Some banks use AI to track activity in people's bank accounts. The technology looks for signs of fraud. Fraud is a crime in which someone lies to take advantage of another person. One way people commit fraud is by stealing people's banking information, such as their credit card numbers. They then use this information to buy things with their victims' money. AI can help banks handle these acts. The AI system alerts banks and customers about potential acts of fraud.

AGRICULTURE AND AI

The use of AI in agriculture is growing. AI can analyze weather patterns to let farmers know when to plant crops. AI can also recommend which crops are best to plant in a given area. Farmers may even use AI to power their tractors. In 2022, the company John Deere announced that it had made a self-driving tractor. The tractor uses AI to steer through fields without a human driver. Using this tractor could save time for farmers.

Banks also use AI to help with customer service. Some banks use chatbots to help customers solve problems online. Chatbots are computer programs that can have humanlike conversations with people. Chatbots study a very large amount of text from books, the internet, and other sources. Their AI learns to recognize and create text in human languages. That way, when people type in a question, chatbots can come up with an answer. Banks use chatbots so customers can ask questions at any time of the day.

Some companies use chatbot programs to handle simple questions and requests, but they use human representatives for more complex issues.

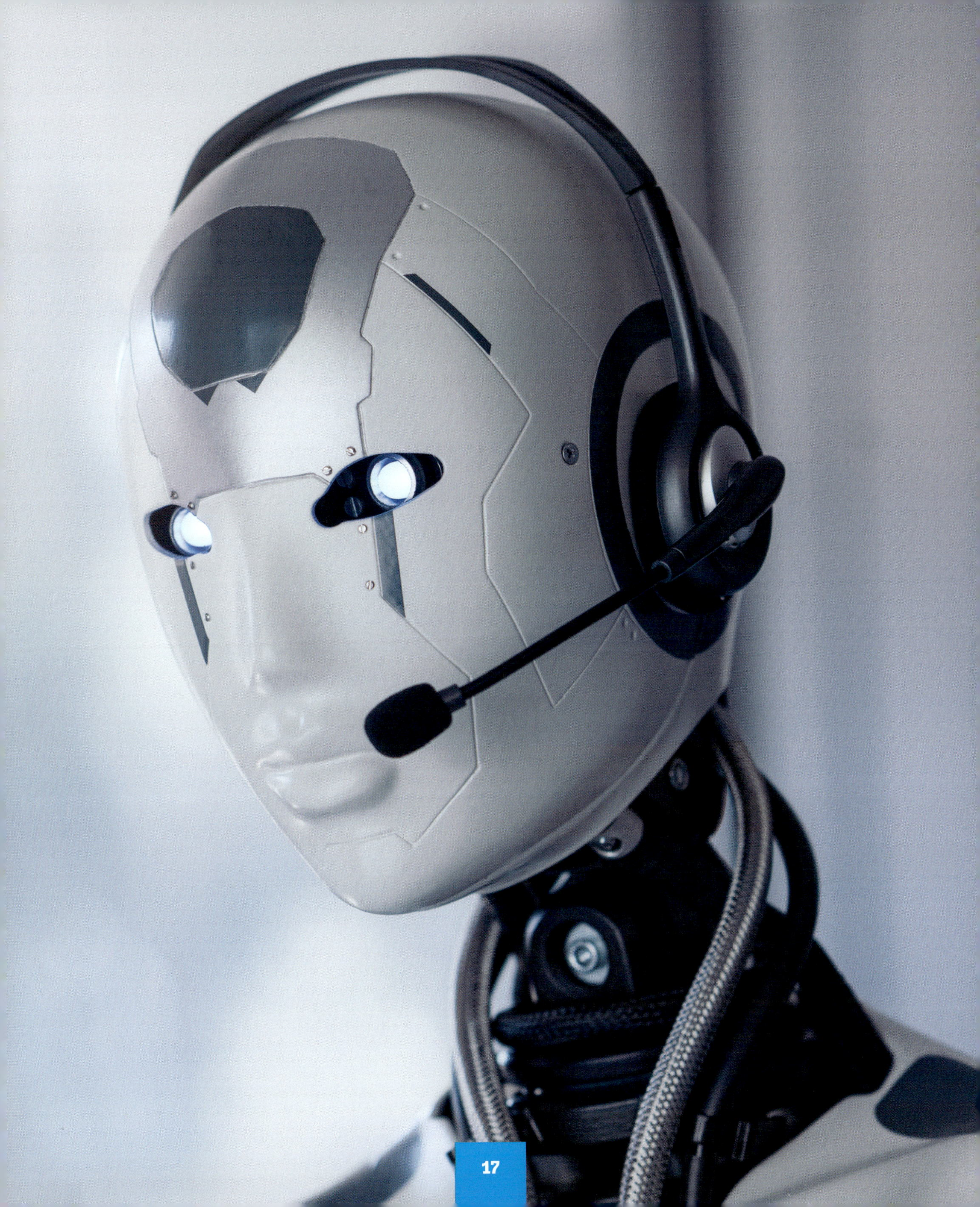

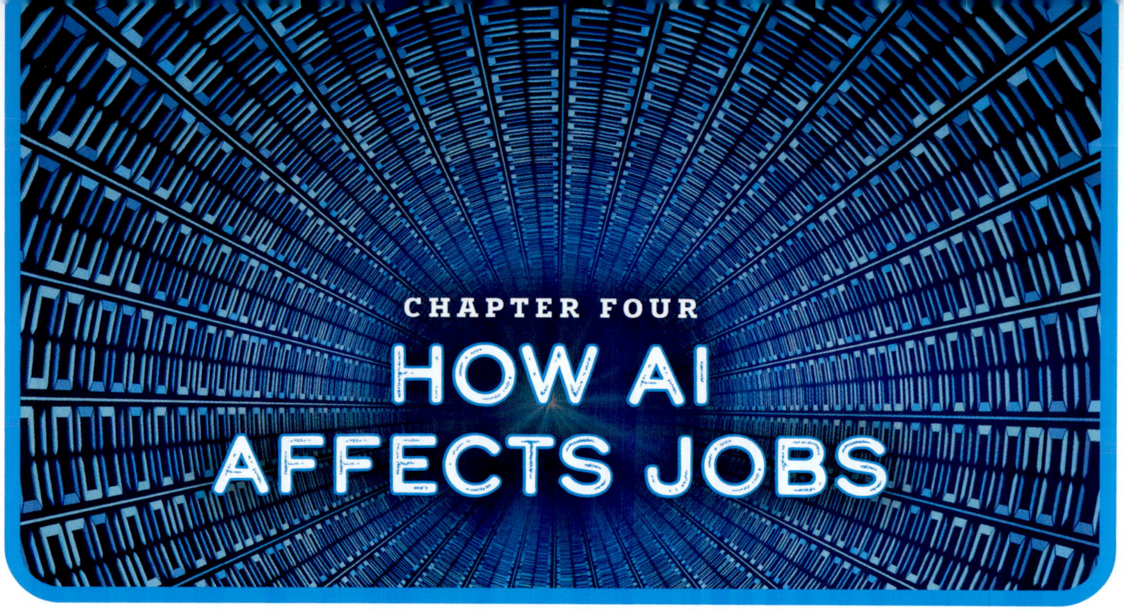

CHAPTER FOUR

HOW AI AFFECTS JOBS

AI can bring huge benefits to companies. However, many people worry about the effects of AI on people's jobs. One study showed that two out of every three US jobs could be affected by AI. Experts do not think every job will be affected by AI. But some jobs are more likely to be replaced by AI than others.

AI is affecting the jobs of customer service representatives. People with this job answer questions and handle requests from customers. Online chatbots can perform these tasks, too. These systems do not need breaks as humans do. This means they can always be available for customers. This has led many companies to replace some of their human workers with chatbots.

WHICH INDUSTRIES ARE MOST EXPOSED TO AI?

Industry	US employees exposed to AI
Office and administrative support	46%
Architecture and engineering	37%
Sales	31%
Farming, fishing, and forestry	28%
Education and library services	27%
Food preparation and service	12%
Construction and resource extraction	6%
Installation and maintenance	4%

This table shows how workers in various industries are exposed to AI. AI can handle many tasks done by workers in office and administrative support. It cannot handle most tasks done in the installation and maintenance industry.

AI might also affect car and truck drivers. This is due to the rise of automated, or self-driving, cars. Self-driving cars do not need a driver. Instead, they use cameras to capture the world around them. The AI looks at the images taken by the cameras. It uses this data to make safe driving decisions on its own.

Fully self-driving cars are not yet available for regular people to buy. But people are working on making these cars a reality. If vehicles continue to become automated, millions of people could lose their jobs. In 2022, about 3.5 million people in the United States worked as truck drivers. That same year, about 5.4 million people worked for the driving service Uber. Some of these workers worry about the future of their field of work.

ART AND GENERATIVE AI

Generative AI is a type of AI that produces content. This includes text, images, and audio. Many people worry about how generative AI will affect artists and writers. This tool allows anyone to create art or write text very quickly. Some companies use generative AI to create content. Critics say the technology threatens the jobs of human artists and writers.

The company Waymo offers self-driving taxis that can take people to their destinations. However, Waymo cars only operate in parts of certain cities, such as San Francisco, California.

The rise of AI will have benefits and drawbacks for workers. Some workers will find that AI makes their jobs easier and faster. Other workers will lose their jobs to AI. People will need to adapt to AI technology as it becomes more common in the workplace.

GLOSSARY

algorithms (AL-guh-rith-umz) Algorithms are step-by-step instructions used to solve a problem or perform a task. AI developers create algorithms that make AI programs perform certain tasks.

analyze (AN-uh-lyze) To analyze something means to study it in detail. Data scientists are people who collect and analyze data.

automated (AW-tuh-may-tid) Something that is automated is able to act without human control. Automated cars could replace human drivers in the future.

data (DAY-tuh) Data is information collected for a purpose. Machine learning AI studies data to learn how to perform a task.

diagnose (dye-ig-NOHSS) To diagnose a medical condition means to recognize what is causing it. AI is used in health care to help doctors diagnose diseases in patients.

efficient (eh-FISH-unt) Efficient means working in a way that gets a job done while using less energy. Companies use AI to make some tasks more efficient.

engineers (en-juh-NEERZ) Engineers are people who use science to design, invent, and build things in order to solve problems. Some people who work in the AI field are machine learning engineers.

industries (IN-duh-streez) Industries are groups of businesses and organizations that produce similar products. Many industries use AI to help them perform certain tasks quickly and easily.

sensors (SEN-surz) Sensors are devices that detect information from the real world, such as light or heat. Robotic waiters have sensors that let them know when food is on their trays.

FAST FACTS

- AI is technology that allows computers to do things that are normally done only by people.
- Many industries use AI to help make certain tasks faster and easier to do. AI technology could help increase productivity around the world.
- Some people have jobs improving AI systems. They include AI developers, machine learning engineers, and data scientists.
- Health care providers can use AI to help diagnose medical conditions of patients. AI robots can also assist doctors during surgeries.
- The banking industry uses AI technology in several ways, including providing customer service and tracking fraudulent activity.
- Studies show that AI could affect two out of every three US jobs. Some of those jobs include customer service representatives and car and truck drivers.

ONE STRIDE FURTHER

- What is machine learning? How is machine learning used in different jobs or industries?
- Come up with two examples of tasks that you think AI could do better than human workers. Why do you think AI would be better?
- Do you think AI will eventually replace all human jobs? Explain why or why not.

FIND OUT MORE

IN THE LIBRARY

Kelly, Christa. *Benefits of Artificial Intelligence*. Parker, CO: The Child's World, 2025.

Kulz, George Anthony. *Artificial Intelligence and the Changing Job Market*. San Diego, CA: BrightPoint, 2025.

Schwartz, Heather E. *Medical Artificial Intelligence Breakthroughs*. Rochester, MN: Mayo Clinic Press Kids, 2024.

ON THE WEB

Visit our website for links about jobs and artificial intelligence:
childsworld.com/links

Note to Parents, Caregivers, Teachers, and Librarians: We routinely verify our web links to make sure they are safe and active sites. So encourage your readers to check them out!

INDEX